So You Want to Start Running...Again!

A Beginner's eBooklet for Tips and Suggestions to Get Running Again

By Jeff Stevenson, Neo-Runner,
Blogger for Runnerstips.net
And CEO of Runnerslog.com

So You Want to Start Running...Again!
A Beginner's eBooklet for Tips and Suggestions to Get Running Again

Copyright © 2011 by Jeff Stevenson

Sabre Enterprises, LLC
8314 W. Pamela St.
Boise, ID 83714
www.sabre-ebooks.com

ISBN 978-0615574608

Sabre-eBooks.com

Table of Contents

Forward 1

Dedication... 3

Special Thanks 3

Chapter 1: It's Never Too Late to Start!.................... 5

Chapter 2: Visit a Physician…..................................... 7

Chapter 3: Choose a Running Program...................... 9

Chapter 4: Keep a Running Log................................ 13

Chapter 5: Regular Workouts 15

Chapter 6: Set Goals and Celebrate Progress 19

Chapter 7: Don't Get Discouraged........................... 21

Chapter 8: Combine Exercise with a Proper Diet 23

Chapter 9: Warm Up and Cool Down 27

Chapter 10: Involve Your Family or Find a Buddy.... 31

Chapter 11: They Have Miles There Too................... 33

Chapter 12: Be Prepared for Elevation 35

Chapter 13: Gravity... 37

Chapter 14: Fueling Up *Before or After* Your Run.... 39

Chapter 15: Controlling Your Breathing 41

Chapter 16: Proper Care for Your Equipment 43

Chapter 17: I Am Sorry, Do I Offend 45

Chapter 18: Fulfilling Your Goals…Then What? 47

Chapter 19: Getting Back in the Saddle Again 49

Forward

Let me start by saying this... "I am no expert! I am only writing about my experiences. The opinions expressed here are simply that, *opinions*. I have cited others' work and linked to those sites I found expert information."

In January 2011, I began running again, something I had not done since I was in high school 25 years ago. I know am not alone in my quest to get back into shape at age 45. My goal is here is share some running tips that helped me get back into running. This book is written for persons, like me, who have recently become aware of their need for more physical fitness activity in their lives . I hope that you enjoy this booklet and find it helpful.

Much of the information in this booklet can be found online and at any number of resources. However, I have put a lot of thought and time into including my personal experiences in this booklet as well in the hopes that others are able to have similar successful experiences as a benefit of your individual efforts. I hope to encourage and perhaps inspire others to start or restart running...again!

Jeff Stevenson
Neo-Runner
Blogger for Runnerstips.net
CEO of Runnerslog.com

Runnerstips.net

Read more about Jeff's experiences on his blog, Runnerstips.net and visit Runnerslog.com to log your activities for FREE!

Dedication

This booklet is dedicated to my wife Tina and my children Vashti, Lucas and Ethan (Hank). You all served to inspire me to be a better person, Husband and Father. I love you all, God Bless.

Special Thanks

I would like to thank all those that assisted in writing this book. I wish to give a special thanks to Coach Steve Blake of Boiserunwalk. Without his instruction and encouragement I would not have been able to accomplish what I have. Thanks Steve

Runnerstips.net

Chapter 1: It's Never Too Late to Start!

In my case, I hadn't run or really exercised for that matter, in several years. In fact, I couldn't remember the last time I had run. But as my weight peaked at over 205 lbs., I knew I needed to do something. So, I began an exercise routine by riding a stationary bike 5 to 7 days per week. After the New Year, I joined a running club (Boiserunwalk) that was having a winter training deal (I will tell more about this in a later chapter).

In high school, I ran track for Carterville High School in Carterville, IL. It really was the only sport I felt like I was built for. You see I am 64 inches tall and as my father would put it "built like a brick outhouse". I have always had very strong legs though and when I ran, there were not too many that could keep up with me. I only ran sprints and for the longest time I had it in my head I wasn't built to run distance or anything beyond a quarter mile. My track coach, Steve Lively, always push me to run longer distances; however, I was stubborn and wouldn't run any longer than 440 meters.

Runnerstips.net

When I went into the Army, at age 30, I trained to run 2 miles in under 15 minutes. This was a hard task to master since it had been such a long time I had run. . And, in the Army, you don't have the luxury of saying "No." - You do it or else. After 14 weeks of training, I ran 2 miles in 14:04 on my last physical training test - the fastest I had ever run 2 miles. Today, at the time of this publication, I run 6 miles in just over 1 hour. Roughly, 10 sustained minutes per mile. Many of you may say that isn't very fast, but for me personally, and an unbelievable personal achievement.

You hear a lot of marketing cliques telling you to "Just Do it", "No Pain No Gain" and so on. There is some truth to this; however, at some point. You will need commit yourself to running or exercising and stick to it.

Here is my advice..."Do this for yourself and only yourself. You'll free good about any progress you make."

Chapter 2: Visit a Physician...

This suggestion is really a no brainer. If you haven't exercised in a while, consult your physician to ensure you are healthy enough for physical activity, plain and simple. Especially if you are fall into any of the following categories, like I did.

Trust me. I'm a doctor.

- Age 40 or over—if you're over age 40 and starting to exercise for the first time, your physician may want you to have an electrocardiogram (EKG) and an exercise stress test to ensure that there are no heart or lung issues that could limit your activity.
- Currently inactive or raising your activity level—If you're currently an active person but are planning to step up your exercise routine, such as going from a casual jogger to a marathon runner, an evaluation is recommended as well.
- Significantly overweight
- Someone with a history of heart problems or a chronic medical condition such as diabetes
- Are new to a sport or exercise program
- Have known health issues
- Have had past injuries

Your physician will likely evaluate your medical history, present level of activity, blood pressure, pulse rate and perhaps conduct blood and urine tests and/or other inform you of any other risk factors. A Physician may wish to review and assess your current medical condition and history, including any surgeries, illnesses or injuries you have had, i.e., heart disease, cholesterol levels.

Discuss any health concerns you have with your health care provider. If your physician recommends specific limitations, follow his or her advice carefully. After all, the idea of increasing activity is to improve your physical health and overall well-being, not cause undue stress and injuries.

Once you've received the go-ahead from your physician, it's wise to start any new exercise program in moderation. Slow but steady progress is preferable to over exertion. One day a week, one hour; two days a week, two hours, etc. would be a great way to begin your program based on your level of health.

Chapter 3: Choose a Running Program.

If you are a person new to running or returning to the sport of running, what kind of a running club or program should your choose? For me it was very simple. I found one that met my budget. I actually got a coupon for a discounted winter training session and took advantage of it. It turned out to be a great group and one that I will continue to stay in contact with. However, some individuals may decide getting involved in an organized running club is less desirable.

I recommend finding a running program that is geared to your specific goals. If you are a

Finding a Running Club in your area

1. You can check with your local running stores. They usually have a good line on the various groups in your area and might be involved in several themselves.

2. Ask your friends that run who they recommend.

3. Search the Internet. Many running clubs have their own websites or blog sites to promote them.

beginning runner, you don't want to run with a group of professional tri-athletes. I chose Boiserunwalk. I chose this program because the

Runnerstips.net

program offered was varied. It included a great cross-section of people from beginner runners to seasoned veterans. Boiserunwalk provides coaching and helpful information on the do's and don'ts of running/walking. We started out on a short run/walk; our first week was one mile.

As a consumer you need to ask yourself the important questions like; "am I a hard-core athlete or just a weekend warrior?" You don't want to get involved in a group that is primarily hard-core competitors if you just want to jog. Here are a few other suggestions:

1. **Find a Club in your area** - Running clubs have a weekly workout at a track somewhere and one or two longer runs that are either on trails or in nearby running venues. Joining a club that is close in proximity will help ensure you to get to the destination for the training making it more likely to stick with it. The best example I can give is the group I belong to. My first session was a winter session and some mornings it was cold, windy, sometimes rainy and snowy. However, since it was at a convenient location, I went every weekend.

2. **You Like the Coach** - The coach and other leaders of the running club are key in your decision to become and stay a member. Are you comfortable with their style of teaching and ability to make everyone feel welcome.

10

Are they happy and patient working with beginners? Does their training approach dovetail with your needs as a runner? How well do they motivate their seasoned runners? Most running clubs will let you do a workout or two with them before you join; go and make sure you get all your questions answered before you sign up.

3. **They Work Different Levels** - Lots of positive or negative things happen during a runner's life. A beginner can work their way from the back of the pack to the front . An elite or experienced runner can have an injury that takes months to recover. The important thing to remember is make sure your running club coaches can work with everyone at the level where they are. As you become a seasoned runner you'll really appreciate the flexibility of coaches that can work with you and your needs.

4. **Do they race and do you care** – For some, racing is fun. Races give you war stories to talk about and serve to motivate you toward your next goal. At the least it should be the kind of group where you can say, "Hey there's a 5K two towns over next weekend. Anyone want to run it with me?" It's a great way to build friendships and to keep you happily running on the road.

5. **Do they encourage Cross-Training** – As a runner you will greatly decrease your

Runnerstips.net

chances of injury if you cross-train. Make sure your running group promotes extracurricular activities such as weight lifting, cycling or other forms of cardio to keep runners healthy. Lots of individuals only want to run. If that's you, you may need a nudge in other directions to keep you strong and healthy. For example, cross-training is one of the most important training skills you can have to keep you healthy and motivated.

6. **Access to good medical information and staff** - Injuries do happen to runners. It helps if your coach and other leaders of the club know good fitness expert people to refer you to if something does happen. A good orthopedist, physical therapist, or massage therapist can really speed your recovery. The club managers should also be happy to work within any medical limitations you have as such as no sprints for two weeks if you are recovering from an injury.

Finding a training program that works for you and gives you what you need in the beginning will make all the difference in the world.

Chapter 4: Keep a Running Log

Most logging sites and software programs allow you to track a variety of things. Some let you upload your maps and GPS coordinates. Some link with social media and allow you to update your Facebook or Twitter accounts with your activity logs.

There is one option for keeping a log. Runnerslog.com is a great free website that has been around since 1999. Runnerslog.com allows members to log miles from anywhere with an internet connection. This site is adding many new features in an upcoming redesign; for example, event registration and a running store.

Runnerslog.com enables you to build a personal profile and keeps track of all your logged information. Track your shoe mileage, locations of

Runnerstips.net

your runs, times of day, conditions at run time and so on.

Whatever fitness option you pick (i.e. running, walking, swimming, bicycling, etc.) keeping a log provides you with an accurate progress report. I use this option frequently and I highly recommend doing this.

Chapter 5: Regular Workouts

If you have been out of the loop for a while, like I had been, working into the regular workouts can feel like a daunting task. I suggest picking something simple to start with. Boiserunwalk started us on a one mile run/walk. I surprised myself by making it all the way through that on two occasions – flat land and hilly terrain. Both were a challenge since I hadn't run any kind of long distance runs in quite some time.

One thing that I had done was working out on a stationary cycle in my home. This beginning activity helped me begin to get some regular motion in my body. An important part of this early beginning included stretching and warming up before I began any physical activity.

So how long does it take to establish an exercise routine that turns into a habit? I recently read an article in Psychology Today that shed some light on this question.

The article called *Creatures of Habit, Effective Advice for Lasting Habit Change*
By Ian Newby-Clark, stated that "it depends". It depends on what kind of habit you are trying to

establish; what are the benefits to continuing with your bad habit; and how often/automatically do you perform the bad behavior?"

What do I mean when I say try to establish a good running behavior habit? First, I found it best to establish an easily attainable goal, on that was measurable. At first, establish a simple goal that is feasible to achieve. For example, my initial goal was to walk or run 2 miles my first week and then slowly add additional miles as the weeks progressed such as a 2 mile run/walk on two different Saturdays; progressing eventually up to a 7 mile run/walk over a 14-week period. I structured my exercise program holding to an every other day schedule sticking with a gradual approach of adding miles; thus, benefitting my physical needs. This way, I had less of a chance of injury and I brought my body up to speed in a way that progressively reinforced the fitness habit goal I set.

Are their any benefits of continuing wrong fitness habits especially when you recognize that these habits can affect your health and well-being? I have a family member who continually complains about their wrong physical habits, and yet, nothing is done to change the habit even though the outcomes may be detrimental. It may be that they just don't know how or what to do different. That is one of the benefits of becoming a member of a running club - to become educated and learn about how/what to do to get started and avoid injury. .

Here is my recommendation to get started. If you have a stationary bike, treadmill, or elliptical machine, place it in the living room by your TV so you can watch your program and exercise at the same time. Eventually, you could generate energy and motivation to expand your workout environment to include the outdoors. .

I know from experience the key to changing unhealthy fitness habits is learning healthy fitness habits and repeating them on a regular bases – lets say at least 3 times a week for a start. While this is not my preference, finding someone to partner with can be a helpful motivator as well.

Runnerstips.net

Chapter 6: Set Goals and Celebrate Progress

For me, the thought of running one mile, let alone several, is something I celebrated. I set two goals when I started the Winter Training Program with Boiserunwalk. The first goal was to get in shape – meaning losing weight, inches and increasing my cardiovascular capacity and physical strength. My second goal was to be able to run a 10K at the end of my training. When I was in high school I ran track. But, because of my self-described physical structure, "short and squatty", I only ran short distances. And over time, I began to put into my head that I just wasn't built to run long distances. I was a sprinter, and sprinters don't need a lot of stamina, I thought. Oh how wrong I was. So the 10K goal was just to prove to myself that I could do it and live to tell the tale.

Something else that I decided was to not keep track of time. My goal was to finish, and it doesn't really matter to me if I am first or last, just that I finish. Now this theory may not work for everyone,

but it takes a lot of pressure off me. Running has become an enjoyable pursuit, not a competitive one.

Achieving a set goal made my effort that much easier. I reached my goal by running 6.2 miles two months before I had intended. I still plan to participate in a 10k race. Knowing I can do it makes my finishing that much better. Now I am setting a new goal. My new goal is to keep myself honest. By that I mean, keep running and continue to improve my physical fitness. I set a goal of running three times per week and at least 5 miles each run. Again I am not interested in how much time it takes, but my mileage and location will be logged on Runnerslog.com.

I celebrated reaching this goal when I completed my first 10k run in June by raising my hands at the finish and quietly praised to myself in my heart and mind. "Job well done, Jeff. You did it!"

Chapter 7: Don't Get Discouraged

Exercise alone doesn't change things overnight. I have been working on my improved fitness and goals for 9 months.

My fitness goals include a balance of better eating habits and exercise. I have discovered as I get older it takes longer. I started in December of 2010. My weight loss goal won't be met until possibly August of 2011. My running goal was met in May 2011, when I ran my first 10K.

Without hard work and perseverance I cannot expect to meet my goals. There are many days that I get up and think "I don't want to ride the stationary bike," but I go into my office and before I

Create a List of Affirmations

1. I deserve and take time to exercise.
2. I enjoy the energetic and trim body I create through exercise.
3. I improve my body one day at a time.
4. It is never too late to improve my body and health.
5. I turn my body into a fat burning machine through healthy eating and exercise.
6. I love and appreciate my body. Like a sculptor, I clearly see the healthy me within.
7. I can taste success every time I drink water.

know it, I am riding. I have found that a great many things in my life are that way. I may initially not want to do them, but once I get started, I have no problem finishing and I have reaped the benefits.

Author's note: Expect a rollercoaster. You will go up and down during your individual programs, remember it is natural to fluctuate. Weight loss is not an overnight experience and healthy weight loss is considered 1-3 pounds per week. Don't get wrapped up in it and keep a positive mental attitude that will carry you to completion.

Chapter 8: Combine Exercise with a Proper Diet

When it comes to eating the proper diet, I have to say I haven't always eaten healthy. I found it hard to put down the tasty foods like pizza, pasta, cheeseburgers, ice cream, etc. I could go on and on but to tell the truth it is making me hungry. As I look back on my eating habits, I discovered I didn't eat bad foods, but I ate way too much of what I was eating. As American's we are programmed via advertising and the media to eat hearty portions. Restaurant portions

Healthy Foods

Unhealthy Foods

considered normal by Americans feed an entire family by European standards. I have never been to Europe, but I know people that have visited and lived there. Europeans eat small portions with many courses, I am told, which include fresh vegetables, fish, chicken rather than processed foods sold in our grocery stores and served in America restaurants.

I am reading a book by Susanne Summers called *Eat Great, Lose Weight*. In it she talks about not just what you eat, but what combinations of foods you consume at a meal. I recommend reading it, because while some of the suggestions are a bit different from what you may have learned as a child, they do make a lot of sense. Combinations of foods have ways of affecting the digestive system in most people. So it is important to examine those combinations if you weight loss results aren't what you feel they should be. Examining and changing your eating habits is the first place to start.

I have dieted on several occasions. Weight Watchers, South Beach, etc. and not one of them produced the results I had hope for. One really successful program I've experienced has been with the Positive Changes Hypnosis Centers. Positive Changes is a behavior modification program that uses hypnosis to helps individuals modify unhealthy eating behaviors into healthier behaviors. While this program may not be for everyone, I actively participate in this program and have had measurable success because the changes have been internalized and become healthy habits. I feel confident because of the success I've had that this is a permanent change and weight loss. This program also reinforces the importance of regular exercise – a balance of healthy eating and exercise. A combination reinforced throughout the program and the results have been dramatic for me.

Conversely, when my first son was born 7 years ago, I went to the gym 5 days per week. I lifted, did cardio and ran some, but I didn't lose a pound. Why? I wasn't changing my eating habits. I figured like so many others, that because I was working out I was burning all these calories. Not entirely true. It is only when I combined healthier eating habits (smaller portions) with dedicated exercise that I got the best results.

Runnerstips.net

Chapter 9: Warm Up and Cool Down

There are many schools of thought when it comes to warming and cooling down – whether you stretch before or after you run. I have read a few articles and here is what I learned. If you stretch before you run and stop, you are 40% more likely to get an injury. If you didn't stretch before they ran, it didn't seem to affect them either way. I stretch before and after I run.

According to some authorities, the main purpose and benefit of warm up exercises is to slowly increase your heart rate. This increase in heart rate helps to raise your body temperature and to increase the blood flow to your muscles.

This increase in blood flow properly oxygenates your muscles and prepares them for the upcoming more strenuous aerobic exercise. When your body is properly warmed up, you can easily and safely perform the needed stretching exercises to ensure proper flexibility and range of motion for your exercise routine.

Warming up properly and then stretching readies your muscles for the aerobic exercise which helps minimize potential muscle tears and injury. A proper warm up exercise and stretching routine increases the elasticity and flexibility of the tendons and ligaments. Your joints are lubricated with

Runnerstips.net

synovial fluid which is released during your warm up routine.

There are articles on the net about stretching before or after runs. In all that I have read and seen, there is no correlation that says if you stretch before you run you will get fewer injuries. In fact, in one article reported in *The Daily Mail*, a UK based publication indicated that, "scientists have revealed warming up before you run does not prevent injury."

The report further stated, "if you already include a stretch in your routine, you shouldn't suddenly stop." Scientists say while priming the muscles doesn't prevent or causes injuries you could hurt yourselves if you switch your technique."

To read more about these scientific finds go to: http://www.dailymail.co.uk/health/article-1357914/A-good-stretch-running-DOES-NOT-prevent-injury.html.

Some of these warm up exercises will work better if you have a friend or a wall you can prop up against. The amount of time you need to properly warm up should be about 5 to 10 minutes, depending on your physical needs. If your body is already somewhat warmed up from some active tasks, then you may only need 5 minutes to properly warm up your body and oxygenate your muscles. However, if you have been sedentary for a while you may want to take 10 minutes to properly warm up. Suggestions:

- Jumping Jacks
- Shoulder Rotations
- Hip Rotations
- Knee Rotations
- Leg Swings
- Ankle Rotations

Once you have finished warming up, think about how you will start running. It is recommended that you don't go out too fast in the beginning. There are a couple things that affect me if I don't warm up and then go out too fast. One; injuring myself and secondly, I tire myself too early and then I struggle through my everyday workout. I ease myself into my workout, whatever it may be. I've found the benefits are greater.

What are the benefits of cool down exercises? Cooling down after exercise means that I gradually reduce the level of activity, and then stretch my muscles. How does it help?

- My heart rate and breathing to return to normal levels.
- Keeps the blood circulating bringing oxygen and nutrients to the muscles and ligaments.
- Helps to remove lactic acid and other waste products from the muscles which can build up during vigorous activity.

Runnerstips.net
- May prevent the muscle soreness which sometimes follows exercising.
- Improves the range of movement in my joints.
- Allows me time to mentally unwind.

Cool down exercises help the heart and breathing to return normal levels after I workout or exercise. Some light activity I do similar to that in my exercise session that is most beneficial includes deep breathing, followed by stretching.

Many people dismiss the cool down as a waste of time, but if you enjoy exercising and want to stay injury free then it's actually very important.

Remember...hydrate, hydrate, hydrate and make sure you replenish your body with a source of energy like nuts, proteins or carbs within 30 minutes of completion.

Chapter 10: Involve Your Family or Find a Buddy

I have to say that it would be nice to involve my family more. However, my wife isn't a runner and my 7 year old said NO! But I do participate with my mother. She doesn't run, she walks. She walks the full distance that I run and I am very proud of her for that. It is encouraging for me to see her make those distances and show up. Really that is the most important thing. My kids may not want to run with me now, but in the future I hope to be a model for them and if they do catch the bug, and I expect to be able to "show up" for them.

As time has gone by my family has found that they enjoy other activities and benefit more from them than running or walking. For example, my mother swims every day and at 70 years old does a minimum of 51 laps in a pool. I applaud her for this, it isn't something I am currently capable of doing. The important thing to me is I am motivated to put more efforts into my quest for better health, I find that I run more by myself than with anyone and I'm comfortable with that. However, I know my family supports me, if not physically; in spirit. In fact my wife Tina has noticed

on days that I might be frustrated that it is okay to "kick me" out for a run. She realizes that I work out my personal issues in better ways than I do if I just sit around and stew over them at home. I run at least 2 to 3 times per week now.

Part of my legacy in my life, is to model the benefits of working and living as healthy a life as I can. Ones health includes their physical, mental and spiritual well-being. Changing my eating and exercise habits are doing this for me.

Chapter 11: They Have Miles There Too...

How many times have you gone somewhere and foregone your running routine. I have learned something over the past few weeks with Boiserunwalk. The greatest tip that I have heard to date when people use the excuse they are traveling or will be out of town to participate in the Boiserunwalk is this..."**They have miles there too**".

There is really no reason that you can't pack your shoes and running gear in order to keep up on your routine. You can map your run with either your smart phone or internet and with the various phone apps. I use Runnerslog.com to log my miles from where ever I am and a new droid phone app is coming out pretty soon and I am excited to use it.

Now I think about where I am going, grab my smart phone and quickly look at Google maps to see what areas I can go for a run or walk. The photos attach show the West Mountain Loop where I run nearly Lake Cascade in Idaho.

Remember, "they have miles there too" so don't be afraid to use them.

Runnerstips.net

Chapter 12: Be Prepared for Elevation

Last winter I decided to "find my miles in a different location". We traveled 105 miles to my in-laws cabin in the mountains of Idaho. There is 3 to 3.5 feet of snow on the valley floor in some areas and the temperature was a brisk 30 degrees. Still, I wanted to get a run in on Saturday morning. Normally, I run at an elevation of about 2800 feet, so running 6 miles wouldn't present too many issues, aside from the normal fatigue that I experience. The family cabin is located near a mountain lake and at the base of West Mountain, the elevation is approximately 4200-4500 feet. I thought that a difference of 1400-1700 feet would not make too much difference, but I was mistaken.

If you are not used to the difference and go out at your normal pace, it will most certainly make a difference in the way you perform. For example, when I was in the Army at basic training at Fort Knox, KY, we

35

were required to run 2 miles in a given time, based on our age group. I had been running at home prior to leaving for basic so I felt prepared for that. However, since the elevation at Fort Knox, KY (751 feet) and the elevation in Idaho are so different I was able to run stronger because my lung capacity was greater at lower elevations. But when I went out for my Saturday run last weekend in a higher elevation, my lungs were not totally prepared. It took half my run to get my lungs accustomed to the change. I still made my run, but it took a lot out of me.

Stew Smith, a contributor for Military.com and Runnerslog.com has written a many articles on high altitude training. Here is one that I have found to be a great source of information. High Altitude Training

So what is the lesson here...for me it was that if I want to continue to run at the higher elevations from time-to-time, I needed to be better prepared for the changes. Preparation is the key to any athletic endeavor. As my running coach says, "everyone can run a marathon; it just might take you several days to finish."

Chapter 13: Gravity

I have found that there are many techniques to running uphill and running downhill. It is widely known that most runners can have a very negative experience running through a hilly course. Uneven terrain presents as many problems to the recreational runner as it does to the seasoned runner.

It may look like the uphill and downhill running techniques are different, but in reality this is not so. It is still running under the same force influence of gravity, however your running technique has a slightly different interaction with gravity

Adjusting your running style to your Surroundings

1. Get comfortable with the perception of a shorter stride.

2. It may be necessary to increase your stride frequency.

3. Resist the temptation to push-off...just pull the feet from the ground.

depending on your direction of travel. The same can be said of running on uneven terrain, because the runner's techniques may be adjusting for the specific trail requirements. Your flexibility to adjust to your surroundings will make the experience a better one.

So this past weekend, I did my Boiserunwalk run...6 miles on the hills. Shaw Mountain Road is part of one of the hardest half marathons around, *The Race to Robie.* The Race to Robie is not only one of the hardest races, but one of the hardest to get into. This race sold out 2,200 participants in about 20 minutes. It was amazing.

Anyway, I ran 3 miles in and 3 miles out and the first 1.5 miles is uphill. Aside from walking a little on the way up I was able to make the whole distance. So what does this have to do with "Gravity"? Well, after you go the first 1.5 miles you have about .25 or so of downhill and then another 1.25 uphill till the three mile mark. So I have been trying to figure out the best way to tackle the going up and down hills. I decided that when I am running downhill, it is best to let gravity have its way.

I felt good just letting the hill pull me down the hills which allowed me to have more energy to run up the hills. Then on the last 1.5 miles, I was able to just breeze down the hill and have the energy to finish the run strong.

Sir Isaac Newton had the right idea...Oh yeah and don't forget to log your miles on runnerslog.com.

Chapter 14: Fueling Up *Before or After* Your Run

One important thing I've discovered is to remember when doing any athletic activity is to fuel your body either before or after you have exercised. When you visit any running store, you will find a wide variety of quick energy products like GU, PowerBars, ClifBars, ClifShots, Gatorade Endurance, Nathan Catalyst Electrolyte Drink Mix, Hammer Gel, Moons & Mojo Bars, Elete Drops, Athletes Honey Milk, and Sports Beans. I haven't tried them. I choose to go a natural route.

When I run, I have been told to make sure that I get proteins in my system within 30 minutes of finishing my exercise. I also find that if I eat a small amount of food an hour or so prior to the run, I have a sufficient amount of energy to start my exercise. I am certain there are a number of articles on fueling up before or after you exercise and a variety of products that you can "Fuel Up" with.

Honestly, I find what works best for me are the simple things. I eat fresh almonds and Honey Stinger Organic Energy Chews and lots of water. Occasionally, I will eat a banana, or some eggs. Lately, I have gotten into making fruit smoothies in the morning. I start with ice, a juice of some sort, usually orange or cranberry, and I add a banana, strawberries, fresh huckleberries (you could substitute blueberries if huck's are not available) and some Pineapple. I also add <u>Psyllium Husks</u> for some added fiber.

Each individual finds what works best for their individual bodies. I recommend finding the more natural sources of energy first. It is usually less expensive and would be naturally healthier for you.

Chapter 15: Controlling Your Breathing

How do you control your breathing when you run? Do you breathe in and out through your mouth or are you a nose breather? Do you pace your breathing like your run?

Learning to control my breathing didn't take any special equipment or classes. It can begin as early as your next run. I have read several articles about how to breathe while running. One website listed instructions for breathing while running. They include; breathing in and out through your mouth, open your mouth slightly as to imitate a "dead fish", taking short shallow breaths, breath from you belly or diaphragm, check your natural breathing patterns and use your ears to control your breathing.

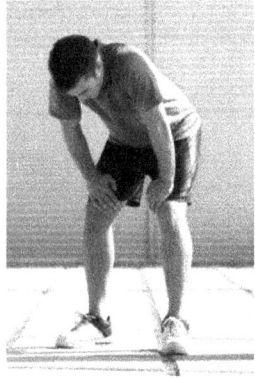

I pace my breathing like I pace my run. I breathe from my mouth, take deep long breaths, breath from my diaphragm and I use my ears. This technique works for me, because I feel like I hyper-ventilate if I take short shallow breaths. I find that I have to concentrate on breathing; I run with my head down and rarely look up to see the distance in front of me. I am unable or unwilling to pace with

41

anyone else while I run. It really makes it difficult for me because then I find I am running at their pace and not my own. In my experience pace and breathing go hand-in-hand. If my pace is too fast, or faster than I normally run, then my breathing will be off pace.

Find a technique that works for you and use it. As time goes on your will most likely refine the technique to be uniquely yours and your athletic efforts will be more enjoyable.

Chapter 16: Proper Care for Your Equipment

Okay so you went out and spent a small fortune on equipment for running from your local running store. The largest expense would be your shoes. If you are running year around, then your shoes will get dirty and possibly even muddy. So what is the proper care for your shoes?

1. If possible, remove the sock-liner or insole and wash it separately. This will help make the inside of your shoe fresher. Laces can be washed or replaced.
2. Surface dirt such as mud and grit can be cleaned off with an old toothbrush or nail brush, a little warm water and a gentle, anti-grease soap. This should take care of the dirt, and is fine to do once in a while.
3. To dry your shoes, don't place them near a heating device such as a radiator. Direct heat will alter the shape of the shoe. Open out the shoe and then stuff the inside with kitchen paper towels or newspaper. The paper will absorb the dampness inside the shoe. A shoe takes about twelve hours to dry out.

Runnerstips.net

By following these simple steps you can make your shoes last longer and smell better.

Chapter 17: I Am Sorry, Do I Offend

Have you ever finished a work out and thought "Holy cow I stink"? I know I have offended, although mostly just myself, since after my run I immediately take a shower. Not long ago, I noticed that I smelled like ammonia after my runs. There was a bit of concern as I wasn't sure why my sweat would take on the odor of a cat box.

I did a little research and here is what I found out.

Our bodies function with a proper balance of Fats, Carbs and Proteins. If that balance gets out-of-wack, then your sweat can range in

The Quick Solution

Cutting the protein and upping the carbs should do the trick, try drinking more water. Water will dilute the ammonia, as well as make it easier to excrete.

Keep in mind too… if an ammonia aroma is emanating from the mouth, is unrelated to sweating and exercise or is accompanied by other severe symptoms; it could be a sign of something serious like severe liver disease or impending kidney failure. A doctor should be consulted ASAP.

smell from industrial strength cleaner and fresh cat urine. I know that isn't a pleasant thought. Fortunately, it is a pretty easy fix.

High-protein, low-carbohydrate diets are generally what lead to sweat stinking of ammonia. Here is how it works. When you begin a diet and then begin to exercise, your body is quickly forced to turn to proteins for the necessary energy. When it does, amino acids are broken down into various components, parts of which are converted into glucose. Other elements that come out of the process are waste products, and if the body can't handle everything being sent its way, the leftovers are excreted out through the skin. Ammonia is one form that ready-to-go waste can take.

Ammonia would be converted into urea and safely expelled through urine. When you have too much ammonia and the body detoxifies in the only other way it can: sweat. An overload of ammonia can impair neurological functions and cause muscle fatigue.

Chapter 18: Fulfilling Your Goals...Then What?

Once you have fulfilled your goal and celebrating that event, then what? In my case, I still had portions of my overall goals to accomplish. I still wanted to lose weight and I also wanted to "keep myself honest". So, I decided to continue with the running club that I joined and to participate in at least 2 more 10K runs. It turns out that I am beginning to enjoy running and exercising. Go Figure...but as of this publication I have lost about 25 lbs. and several inches all over.

Once I run a couple more 10K races I am even considering running a half marathon. Believe me this isn't something I had ever intended when I began this process in January of 2011. Honestly, it was the farthest thing from my mind. As I mentioned in *Chapter 6*, my goal was to get into shape and just run a 10K. However, I have found that I like the feeling of running with others that are in the same mindset as I am. Believe me, I am healthier than I was and I am on the road to even better health because of my physical commitment and involvement.

Chapter 19: Getting Back in the Saddle Again

At some point in your journey you may decide to take a break from your running routine. Depending on where you live there may be a part of the year not friendly to running outside, perhaps you don't not want to brave the cold, or you may be recovering from injury. In any case, eventually, when you want to get back into your running routine there are some ways to start back up without potentially injuring yourself.

1. Staying in touch with your running group, if you belong to one. I continually monitor my groups Facebook page, so that I can see what everyone else is doing. I try to keep in mind that some of these people are a little more hardcore about running than I am, but it does serve as inspirational to me when I see what they are doing.

2. Don't try to go out and run your longest distances. It is better to bring yourself back slowly. This way you can avoid re-injury or ending the new training season early because of a new injury. At the end of my season in September 2011, I was proudly up to 7 miles per run. I had competed in 4, 10K races and my last I took first in my age

group. However, after my break, my starting run was only 2 miles. Of which I walked probably .5 to .75 miles over the course of the 2 miles. This is also a great time to restart tracking your progress again. Visit Runnerslog.com and get your FREE membership today!

3. Don't go out at world record pace! Trying to return at your season end pace will only end in injury, pain and soreness. It is best to apply the attitude of running at a much slower pace than you normally would run. Again, this is a great way to avoid injury.

4. Get your body re-acclimated to your running routine. Think about your breathing techniques and body mechanics. Don't forget to stretch and drink plenty of water.

5. Check your equipment. Now may be a good time to replace those old running shoes, shorts, shirts and any other running items before the season gets going. A great place to get your running apparel is the Runnerslog.com store. They offer great stuff at reasonable prices.

Perhaps your location dictates your routine. Think about exercising in the gym for a few months until the weather is more suitable for outdoor activity. The running club I belong to chooses to start training outside in January, so that those that want to run early season half-marathons are ready. I enjoyed it because I knew at least one day out of the week I was outside getting some much needed exercise.

Whatever plan you have for getting back running after a short break, stick with it. You'll feel better and as the weather gets nicer, you'll be injury free and confident that you can accomplish your loftiest goals. Have a great season!

Runnerstips.net

Stay tuned to my blog at runnerstips.net to see further postings. Log onto Runnerslog.com and start your own running adventure.